131

Connecting
Conversations
for Parents and Teens

How to build a
lifelong bond with your teen!

Jed Jurchenko

www.CoffeeShopConversations.com

Printed by KDP,
An Amazon.com Company
Available from Amazon.com

This book is dedicated to parents
and teenagers who are committed to
connecting, growing, and learning together
in this ever-changing world.

Also By Jed

131 Conversations that Engage Kids

131 Boredom Busters and Creativity Builders

131 Creative Conversations for Couples

131 Engaging Conversations for Couples

131 Creative Conversations for Families

131 Necessary Conversations before Marriage

131 Conversations for Stepfamily Success

Ten Quick Wins for Writers

Coffee Shop Conversations: Psychology and the Bible

Coffee Shop Inspirations: Simple Strategies for Building Dynamic Leadership and Relationships

Bonus Gift!

Thank you for purchasing this book! I would love to send you a free, bonus gift.

Transform from discouraged and burned out, to an enthusiastic agent of joy who leads at a higher–happier–level! *Be Happier Now* is easy to apply and is perfect for parents, stepparents, mentors, pastors, coaches, and friends.

Discover practical strategies for staying energized so that you can encourage and refresh others. This easy-to-read guide will guide you each step of the way!

www.CoffeeshopConversations.com/Happiness

Contents

Introduction

Welcome to *131 Connecting Conversations for Parents and Teens.* The purpose of this short yet potent parenting book is to inspire you and your teenager to connect like never before. This is not merely another volume crammed with the latest parenting advice. Instead, it will assist you in taking massive action. The opening chapters of this book are just for parents and provide research-based connection advice. This is followed by 131 connecting conversation starters, which provide the opportunity to practice these crucial principles with your teen.

Broken down even further, the structure of this book is as follows. Chapter one explores why engaging connections are essential to a healthy, happy, and prosperous development during the teenage years. Chapter two offers practical relationship strategies to support you in engaging like a pro. Chapter three contains 131 conversation starters to assist you in strengthening the bond with your teen. Finally, chapter four addresses some unique relational challenges that teenagers face in our technology-inundated world.

The Power of Engaged Action

I once heard a speaker suggest that most people do not require more information in order to grow. Instead, they would benefit from somebody standing behind them hollering, "Run!" at the top of their lungs. I wholeheartedly agree. Taking action is far more valuable than head knowledge alone. In fact, I believe nearly everyone can drastically improve their lives by merely applying the wisdom they already possess.

As we will see, proactive parenting is especially valuable during the teenage years. Although the majority of parents plan to have significant conversations with their teenagers, many find that life gets in the way. Good intentions get sidetracked by a whirlwind of activities. Other parents procrastinate because actually having those difficult conversations feels so awkward in the moment. Whatever the case may be, one thing is sure. Time passes quickly, and if parents continue to postpone engaging with their teenagers, a vital opportunity to build into their young adult's life will be lost. Happily, this does not need to happen to you.

The conversation starters in this book will equip you to have crucial conversations with your teenager in a creative, highly engaging, and coffee shop casual manner. I wholeheartedly believe that going through these questions will be an enlightening and enjoyable experience for you both. So, grab a cup of coffee, tea, or another favorite beverage as you get ready to embark on this connection adventure!

Sincerely,

COFFEE SHOP CONVERSATIONS

The Power of
Engaged Conversation

Relationships are potent! By proactively connecting with your teenager, you are directly contributing to his or her physical health, personal development, and overall joy. Although small moments of engaged interaction may not seem like a big deal, I assure you they are.

I know this because when I reflect on my teenage years, I can easily recall the adults who built into my life. First, there was a youth pastor, who regularly drove his truck onto our junior high campus to tailgate with us during our lunch break. I especially appreciated his willingness to go beyond the typical spiritual duties of a youth pastor to connect with me in my world.

Then, there was the principal of our small homeschool association who called to see if I was interested in serving as our school's sixth-grade camp counselor. When I said "Yes!" she exclaimed, "Then, you'd better pack your bags fast because the kids are already at camp waiting for their counselor to arrive." Although I enjoyed getting out of a week of schoolwork, the honor of being entrusted with this responsibility is what I remember most. Finally, the summer before my senior year in high school, my parents spent hours driving me back and forth from my first job. Even though I was only serving ice cream cones and hot dogs at the local zoo, their commitment to my success meant a lot. It also instilled in me a value for hard work that persists to this day.

These gifts of time, trust, and support helped me to form my identity. Because adults whom I respected thought that I was capable, caring, and competent, I believed this too. If you reflect on your teenage years, it is likely that you will also recall several adults who connected with you in simple yet profoundly meaningful ways. Upon closer examination, you may discover that these interactions shaped your character and continue to contribute to the person you are today.

Identity Formation

In psychology, object relations theory suggests that teenagers internalize the words and actions of significant people in their lives. This includes parents, teachers, mentors, youth pastors, coaches, and friends. These "voices" pop into their heads at opportune moments and continue to influence them throughout their lifetime.

To better understand this concept, you may want to listen to the song "Voices" by Chris Young. This jaunty country song is comprised of sayings from family members who influenced the singer's life. One of my favorite passages goes like this:

I hear voices like

My dad sayin', "Quit that team
And you'd be a quitter for the rest of your life"
And mama tellin' me to say a prayer
Every time I lay down at night

And grandma sayin', "If you find the one
You better treat her right"
Yeah, I hear voices all the time

Because this song does such an excellent job of demonstrating how object relations theory plays out in real life, I often play it in the psychology classes I teach.

The downside is that teenagers also absorb the negative voices they hear, and they do this faster than a wool sweater soaks up water in a downpour. When damaging words are internalized, they, too, play repeatedly in our teenager's mind. A head filled with negative voices increases anxiety and leads to a host of problems. These harmful voices are also referred to as "stinking thinking" or "head trash." They are so destructive because they are neither helpful nor true.

Identifying Negative Voices

Most teenagers get exposed to a host of negative voices throughout their lifetime. Sometimes the words are spoken aloud. Others are drummed up in our teenager's imagination. Examples of head trash include thoughts like:

- I'm not good enough.
- There is something inherently wrong with me.
- Nobody likes me.
- I am not capable and must look to others to do difficult things for me.
- I am too broken to succeed.
- I am a failure, and I should expect to fail.

Teenagers can be cruel, and shielding our teens from all negativity is impossible. The crucial question is, "What will your teenager do with the negative voices that come his or her way?" Some teenagers carry these damaging beliefs into adulthood. Others learn how to dispute and reject them. The good news is that parents can assist their teenagers in eradicating self-limiting beliefs.

Taking Out Head Trash

On our block, Tuesday is garbage day. On more than one occasion, I have forgotten to take the trash bins out for the collectors. The following day, you might find me standing inside our garbage cans, jumping up and down, in a feeble attempt to smash down the heaping pile of rubbish. Similarly, head trash compiles quickly, and regular garbage days are a must.

Recently, our daughter Brooklyn was attempting to learn how to juggle a soccer ball. This proficiency involves keeping the ball in the air using only one's feet. Brooklyn was not picking up the skill as quickly as she would have liked and blurted out, "I am no good at this." My wife Jenny, who was standing nearby, exclaimed, "What! Is that true?" Then, Brooklyn's older sister chimed in, asserting, "No, Brooklyn is just not good at it yet. She needs more practice first."

Now that is a powerful reframe. Slowly but surely, our kids are learning to take out their head trash by disputing their self-limiting beliefs. The bottom line is teenagers need regular garbage days, and there is much that parents can do to help.

Parenting Hope

The media frequently spotlights the darker side of teenage life. Headlines hone in on gloomy outliers and worst-case scenarios. One goal of this chapter is to offer parenting hope. Although parents cannot protect their teenagers from everything, there is much that we can do. By connecting with your teen on a regular basis, you will become a constructive voice in his or her head. In fact, just by going through the questions in this book, you are nonverbally communicating, "You are important, you are worth spending time with, and your opinions matter!"

Growing Together

For me, this book is personal. As a father of four girls—one who is rapidly approaching her teenage years—I am incessantly searching for innovative ways to deepen the bond with my own kids. This passion is also fueled by the knowledge that youth who regularly engage with their parents are better equipped for life. If you would like more evidence, then keep reading. The remainder of this chapter focuses on three reasons why simple moments of connection create such a profound impact.

Connecting Matters

Close relationships are a vital component of a healthy, prosperous, and happy life.

Science, Scripture, and personal experiences all point to this same conclusion. First, engaged connections enhance a teenager's overall health.

1. *Close connections give teenagers a physical, mental, and spiritual boost.*

According to a meta-analytic review published by *PLOS Medicine*, there is a strong correlation between positive social interactions and mortality risk. The study reveals "a 50% increased likelihood of survival for participants with stronger social relationships."[1] The data suggests that relationship deficits are more hazardous to a teenager's physical health than inactivity or obesity and are on par with excessive alcohol consumption and smoking. This makes me wonder if the teenage years should come with a warning label reading: *Caution, disconnecting from your parents is hazardous to your health.*

Equally as fascinating is a study entitled, *The Impact of Child-Parent Attachment, Attachment to God and Religious Orientation on Psychological Adjustment.*[2] Researchers examined what happens when someone attempts to correct toxic relationship habits by spiritual means alone. The results are messy and challenge the veracity of some common advice given by well-meaning Christians. This includes suggestions to pray more, read the Bible, attend church regularly, and then trust God for the results. While these fundamental spiritual disciplines are foundational to spiritual growth, they are not a magic wand nor a viable solution to all of life's troubles.

Surprisingly, adhering to these ideas alone can actually cause problems to increase. Study participants who sought to heal their relationship wounds through only spiritual means eventually ended up bringing their poor relational habits into their bond with God.

Perhaps this is why James 5:16 says, "Confess your sins to one another and pray for one another so that you may be healed." Attachment problems form through negative human interactions, and they heal during corrective experiences with other human beings.

Because poor connection habits seep into our relationship with our Creator, it is reasonable to assume that positive ones do too. Consequently, by connecting with your teenager in healthy ways, you are equipping him or her with the skills needed to have a healthy relationship with God. This makes bonding with your teenager a decidedly spiritual act. Although the scientific research is new, teachings on the immense value of human bonds are woven throughout Scripture.

2. *Two people are better than one, and close connections help teenagers to succeed.*

Even in today's high-tech world, nobody succeeds alone. Human beings are God-designed to connect, and people generally perform better when others are around. This concept has existed from the beginning of time.

In Genesis 1, shortly after creating Adam, the first man, God enlists him in the original relational experiment—one that is easily on par with relationship studies conducted by Ivy League universities today. While God could have simply told Adam, "You need a partner," instead, He guides Adam in making the discovery for himself.

The experiment begins with God parading every species of animal before Adam. Next, God calls attention to the fact that each creature has a suitable mate. He then asks Adam to identify his female counterpart. When Adam is unable to do so, God causes Adam to fall into a deep sleep and fashions Eve, the first woman, from Adam's side.

After laying eyes on Eve for the first time, Adam proclaims, "This one at last is bone of my bone and flesh of my flesh."[3] In other words, Adam finds what he is looking for and gets God's point: God designed human beings to connect with other humans. Relationships are so significant that God illustrated our need for human connection in an extraordinary way.

Then, around 900 B.C., King Solomon reiterates this point, writing, "Two people are better than one, because they can reap more benefit from their labor. For if they fall, one will help his companion up, but pity the person who falls down and has no one to help him up."[4]

Most parents will be able to relate because young adults fall often. Fortunately, between the ages of 0-18 is the optimum time to fail. Before adulthood, mistakes are expected, support systems are strong, and bouncing back from blunders is about as easy as it gets. Moreover, failures can transform into opportunities for growth when they are accompanied by grace-filled conversations.

Conversing with Truth and Grace

Many questions in this book center on growing from past mistakes. These conversation starters provide opportunities to pick your child's brain, finding out what he or she has already gleaned from these invaluable experiences. They also provide parents with the perfect opportunity to share their own strengths and failures. I highly recommend sharing both, for two reasons. First, teenagers will benefit from learning about the healthy habits that you use to succeed, and this book provides 131 opportunities to pass on these priceless insights. On the other hand, sharing mistakes models vulnerability, honesty, and the ability to bounce back from blunders — which paves the way for your teenager to do the same.

Finally, a mutual sharing of successes and failures is valuable because it leads to *intimacy* or *into-me-see*. Intimacy involves courageously looking inward, and then boldly revealing ourselves to another. In this type of sharing, parents and teenagers exchange glimpses of their inner worlds. This insightful process can be lots of fun, which brings us to the third reason why connecting is so significant.

3. *Engaged connections is a blast!*

What if this is as good as life gets? This unusual thought popped into my head as I cruised down a long stretch of open highway. It was a crisp winter day. A steaming mug of coffee sat in the console to my right, while a favorite music station hummed softly in the background. These long work drives offer an ideal opportunity for thoughtful reflection. On this particular trip, my mind wandered to future adventures.

I imagined how incredible it would be to take my wife, Jenny, on vacation to Hawaii, on a cruise to Alaska, and for the two of us to fulfill her dream of returning to Europe. As I envisioned Jenny and I strolling hand-in-hand down a tropical beach, the daydream consumed me. Suddenly, I found myself listening in on our conversation.

Surprisingly, the two of us were not planning our next escapade but reminiscing about favorite family experiences. We recalled the times our girls took their first steps, learned to ride their bikes, and their joyous laughs as they played with friends in our yard. These seemingly ordinary moments had transformed into our most cherished memories.

What if I will treasure these moments the most? What if right now is as good as it gets? I wondered to myself.

This notion jolted me out of my reveries. Although studies suggest that a couple's overall happiness decreases with the birth of their first child, the many peak moments that come from raising a child are priceless. I imagine that the teenage years are similar. On the one hand, watching one's child transition into adulthood comes with a distinct set of stresses. On the other hand, parents and teenagers will never have this incredible opportunity again. Now is the time to converse, laugh, cry, share wisdom, and build an abundance of happy memories.

While having a blast with your teenager may not sound like a big deal, fun is so essential to a healthy life that the renowned therapist, William Glasser, includes it on his list of five basic human needs. This means that if you and your teenager find yourself bursting into spontaneous laughter, getting lost in conversation, and having boatloads of fun along the way, then the two of you are doing things right. Remember, the ultimate goal of this book is not to complete every single conversation starter. Instead, it is to connect often, to connect deeply, and to become an encouraging voice in your teenager's head.

By now, I hope you are thoroughly convinced that connecting with your teenager is well worth the effort. Not only will this help your teen stay on the right track, but this process can also be an immense joy.

Nevertheless, if this type of proactive engagement sounds intimidating, don't fret. In the next chapter, we will dive into four strategies for connecting like a pro. Then, you and your teenager will have the opportunity to take action with 131 creative, connecting, and crucial conversations!

How to
Connect Like a Pro

Connecting is far more complicated than many people realize. In fact, talking, communicating, and connecting are vastly different, with connecting being the most intricate of the three. Talking is easy because it only requires that one person's lips move. Communicating is more elaborate because it needs a listener who hears and understands the message. Connecting takes this process deeper still, by placing the value of the relationship above all else.

Communicating vs. Connecting

In the past, therapists attempted to help parents and teens improve their relationship by focusing on communication. A standard exercise involved assigning one person the role of speaker and the other the role of the listener. The speaker's job was to convey his or her message clearly. The listener's duty was to attend closely enough to accurately repeat what was said. The speaker would then check for accuracy and reiterate any ideas that were not correctly received the first time. Eventually, the roles of speaker and listener reversed, and the process repeated itself. While there is nothing wrong with this exercise—and I have spoken to a number of families who claim it has been helpful—it can also feel cold and robotic.

Parroting back an opposing viewpoint is difficult, and listeners sometimes find they can tune in with their ears while tuning out with their hearts. One of my colleagues suggests that this process helps people to "argue better." Participants tone down the emotional volume of the conversation but don't necessarily grow closer together. When this happens, a gaping hole forms where the warm bond should be. It is important to remember that God did not create us to debate nicely but to connect deeply.

Connect to Live Better

I once heard an exasperated parent share how his son would not follow directions at home. After exhausting every parenting trick in the book he blurted out, "I know that you don't want to listen, but would you please just do this for me?" Much to his delight, the young man obeyed. This dad went on to report that although rewards, consequences, and reasoning had failed, appealing to their relationship worked nearly every time. Consequently, it was their bond that made all the difference.

If you want to be heard, then talk. If you wish to be understood, then communicate. However, if you desire to influence your teenager in a lasting way, then you must connect. Author, speaker, and business leader, Charlie "Tremendous" Jones said, "You will be the same person you are today in five years but for two things: the people you meet and the books you read." Charlie understands the power of connection. Relationships are a catalyst for growth, and this chapter provides four powerful strategies for developing this type of life-changing connection with your teen.

1. Offer Empathy Often

Empathy involves walking a mile in your teenager's shoes. A quirky friend of mine likes to say, "Empathy is great because if I walk a mile in your shoes, then I will have your shoes and be a mile away!" Of course, this is not the type of empathy suggested.

In true empathy, parents strive to see the world through their teenager's eyes. Empathizing is easiest when parents understand that empathy does not require agreement. Even when teenagers make outlandish mistakes, parents can still identify with their pain.

For example, as a child I made some foolish mistakes. On one occasion, I picked up a bumblebee with my bare hands. Of course, I got stung. Later, I stuck my finger in an electrical socket and received quite the jolt. Although my parents warned me not to do either of these things, I chose to learn the hard way. Both of these events brought me to tears. While my parents could have easily started with "I told you so," they wisely began with empathy. Empathy says, "I see that you are hurting, and I hurt with you."

Empathetic parents put Romans 12:15 into practice. This passage says, "Rejoice with those who rejoice, weep with those who weep," and describes empathy at its best. When you don't know what to say next, start with understanding. When words abound, it is easy to offend, but it is almost impossible to go wrong with empathy.

2. Expect Mistakes

If your teenager makes foolish mistakes, then congratulations, your family is typical. Transitioning from childhood to adulthood is messy, so parents might as well enjoy the ride. Helping teens survive and thrive is easiest if we frame this stage in life as a wonderful, messy, and chaotic adventure.

I am sure my parents will never forget the time my friend brought over his pet king snake, which promptly slithered away and lost itself inside of our house. Then there were the months I unremittingly begged for a pet potbellied pig, because I thought it would be a much cooler pet than a dog. I have no doubt that teenagers are experts at driving their parents crazy.

A favorite image on my blog shows a dad with a goofy look on his face, endlessly spinning a bolt attached to his forehead. The picture resonates with me because I habitually feel like this dad. I am a fixer by nature. This means I have a habit of spinning problems incessantly in my mind, searching for a resolution. My passion to fix is so strong that I can drive my family nuttier than a bag of trail mix with attempts to please everyone.

In psychology, this compulsion to fix is called *the righting reflex.* Parents with an overactive righting reflex passionately try to repair all that is wrong in the world. The downside is that this can include demanding that teenagers do things our way, or what we perceive as "the right way." Demands like this typically damage the relationship. Parents who allow messes and mistakes have learned how to relax their righting reflexes at appropriate times.

The next time you are tempted to argue with your teenager, pause to consider if it might be time to relax your righting reflex and allow your teenager to learn from his or her mistakes instead. After all, growing from personal experiences is how many of us parents learned the invaluable life lessons that we now know so well.

3. Don't pick up the rope.

One of my favorite parenting tools is called, "Don't pick up the rope." While relaxing the righting reflex is about reducing the compulsion to fix, letting go of the rope involves liberating ourselves from the need to have our teenager understand our point of view.

Even the brightest teenager in the world is still just a teenager. No matter how much parents explain themselves, there will always be some things that teenagers will not get. He or she has merely not attained the level of maturity required to understand. Letting go of the rope involves holding on to parenting rules, boundaries, and limits while doggedly refusing to engage in back-and-forth arguments.

Have you noticed that some arguments resemble a game of tug-o-war?

- One person makes a point and the other person counterpoints. Then, the first person tries harder to drive the point home.
- One person shuts down, so the other person shuts down too. Soon, a war of silence begins, with each person determined not to be the one who breaks it.
- A teenager pushes his parent's buttons. The parent threatens a consequence, and the teenager pushes harder, perhaps even responding with a staunch, "I don't care!" in regards to the punishment.

The easiest way to end tug-o-war-like arguments is to avoid picking up the rope in the first place. Parents can decline to enter into escalating disagreements by actively listening, empathizing with their teen's hurts, allowing them to learn from mistakes, and by calmly stating they will think things over before discussing the matter further.

When the amygdala (the brain's fight, flight, or freeze emergency response system) gets triggered, the frontal cortex, or critical-thinking part of the brain, turns off. This makes reaching a reasonable solution nearly impossible. Because it takes a full twenty minutes for an activated amygdala to calm down, allowing your teenager sufficient time to reregulate before returning to the issue is essential.

Happily, you are never obligated to engage in disagreements. You can let go of the rope at any time. The key is to go beyond mere intellectual understanding and to put this powerful connection strategy into practice.

4. Connect Like Velcro.

The happiest relationships are Velcro relationships. If you examine Velcro closely, you will find that one strip contains hundreds of small hooks while the other is comprised of many tiny loops. This system of hooks and loops is what allows Velcro to connect in an almost magical manner.

Over time, the hooks and loops stretch out. Then, when the strips are moved toward each other, they connect while the two pieces are quite a distance away. It is almost as if the hooks and loops reach for each other.

Similarly, in Velcro relationships, two people connect, disconnect, and then reach out for one another. Relationship expert John Gottman uses the term "repair attempts" to describe the reaching phase. A repair attempt is anything that draws two people back together. This might happen through a shared joke, a kind gesture, a gentle touch, or a simple smile.

According to John's research, repair attempts are an essential ingredient in lasting relationships. This is important for parents to know, because right now is the ideal time to help your teenager learn to connect, disconnect, and reconnect well. Not only is this skill important in your own relationship, but it will also benefit your teenager throughout life. Without a doubt, the best relationships are Velcro relationships. The ability to repair a broken connection is a crucial ingredient of happy friendships and lasting marriages.

The conversation starters in the next chapter provide excellent opportunities to put these four fundamental connection skills into action. These conversation starters intentionally start out light, with more serious questions peppered throughout the book. After all, too much intensity at once can feel overwhelming. As you progress through these questions, I wish you and your teenager an abundance of happy connection moments!

131
Connecting Conversations
for Parent and Teens

*Good habits formed at youth
make all the difference.*

~ Aristotle

*Being a teen can be tough.
Just try to surround yourself
with really good friends
that really have your back,
and also be a really good friend
to those who really care about you.
If you're not sure about certain things,
talk to your friends that you trust
and your family.*

~ Victoria Justice

*It takes courage to grow up
and become who you really are.*

~ E. E. Cummings

Conversation #1

Imagine the zoo offers to let you keep one animal as a pet. Which creature do you bring home with you, and why?

Conversation #2

What is your all-time favorite movie, and what do you like about it?

Conversation #3

What movie is so terrible that you would un-watch it if you could? What made this movie so painful to see?

Conversation #4

What is the best birthday present you ever received? What made this gift so special?

Conversation #5

Helen Keller, a woman who overcame a number of adversities, said, "Life is either a daring adventure or nothing." Describe something that makes your life a daring adventure.

Conversation #6

Who is one of your fictional heroes? What do you admire about this person?

Conversation #7

Who is one of your real-life heroes, and what qualities do you admire in this person?

Conversation #8

What is the most trouble you have ever gotten into at school? What is one thing you learned from this experience?

Conversation #9

When teenagers get mad, how can they manage their anger in positive ways?

Conversation #10

When parents are upset, what types of things should they do to cope with their frustrations in constructive ways?

Conversation #11

In your opinion, what is an appropriate age for a teenager to go out on a first date? Why did you choose this age?

Conversation #12

In your opinion, is it better for a teenager to date many different people, have one long-term relationship, or not to date at all? Explain your answer.

Conversation #13

C.S. Lewis said, "Friendship is born at that moment when one person says to another: 'What! You too? I thought I was the only one.'" Who is your best friend? In what ways are the two of you alike?

Conversation #14

What character qualities are most important for a good friend to have? How well do you think you are doing demonstrating these qualities yourself? Explain your answer.

Conversation #15

Bill Gates said, "Most people overestimate what they can do in one year and underestimate what they can do in ten years." What big goal would you like to accomplish ten years from now?

Conversation #16

Imagine that your house is on fire. Fortunately, all of the people and pets are safe. Unfortunately, you only have enough time to grab three personal items before rushing out the door. What do you take with you, and why?

Conversation #17

Who is (or was) one of your favorite teachers? What is something valuable that you learned from this person?

Conversation #18

Which political party do your values most closely align with? What are some primary issues that cause you to associate with this political party?

Conversation #19

Eleanor Roosevelt said, "Do one thing every day that scares you." What is something that scares you? Using a scale of 1-10, with one being "Not very much" and ten being "terrified," rate how frightened this makes you.

Conversation #20

If you could travel back in time and give your younger self one piece of advice, what would it be?

Conversation #21

If you were the appointed president of your country for one day, what law would you enact or change?

Conversation #22

Bruce Lee said, "Simplicity is the key to brilliance." What are three simple pleasures that bring a smile to your face?

Conversation #23

Share three things that you love about your family.

Conversation #24

What is something about your family that frustrates or annoys you?

Conversation #25

What book are you currently reading, and why did you decide to read it?

Conversation #26

Imagine that you get to spend an hour with the president, chatting over coffee. You can ask him/her for counsel or give advice on how you think the country should be run. How will you use this time?

Conversation #27

In your opinion, what is good about being a teenager?

Conversation #28

In your opinion, what makes being a teenager difficult?

Conversation #29

Dr. Seuss said, "Don't cry because it's over, smile because it happened." When was the last time that you felt happy, and what made you feel this way?

Conversation #30

In your opinion, what is good about being a parent? If you are a teenager, what do you think is good about your parent's life?

Conversation #31

In your opinion, what makes being a parent difficult? If you are a teenager, what do you think makes your parent's life challenging?

Conversation #32

What are three wonderful qualities you see in the person that you are going through this book with?

Conversation #33

What is a favorite memory of a time we spent together? What made this particular experience so meaningful to you?

Conversation #34

If your life had a theme song, what would it be? What do you like about this particular song, and how does it portray you?

Conversation #35

Finish this sentence: "In my opinion, a teenager should always _____."

Conversation #36

Finish this sentence: "In my opinion, a teenager should never _____."

Conversation #37

Finish this sentence: "In my opinion, a parent should always _____."

Conversation #38

Finish this sentence: "In my opinion, a parent should never _____."

Conversation #39

When was the last time that you felt sad, and what made you feel this way?

Conversation #40

What do you believe happens immediately after someone dies? Why do you think this?

Conversation #41

Howard Thurman said, "Don't ask yourself what the world needs. Ask yourself what makes you come alive, and go do that, because what the world needs is people who have come alive." What activities make you feel alive? How might you build this passion into a viable career?

Conversation #42

If I wanted to do something simple to make you smile, what should I do?

Conversation #43

If I wanted to do something big to bring you joy, what should I do?

Conversation #44

On a scale of 1-10, with one being incredibly relaxed and ten being overwhelmingly stressed, what is your overall level of stress this week? Explain why you assigned the number you did.

Conversation #45

If you could ask God one question, what would it be?

Conversation #46

If you could eat a meal with any Biblical character, with whom would you dine? Why did you choose this person?

Conversation #47

If you could spend the day with anyone currently alive, who would it be, and why?

Conversation #48

If you could spend the day with any historical figure, whom would it be? What is one thing you would hope to learn from this person?

Conversation #49

On a scale of 1-10, with ten being extremely important and one being not important at all, how significant is your faith to you? Explain why you assigned the number you did.

Conversation #50

Describe your dream job. What would you enjoy about doing this type of work?

Conversation #51

Theodore Roosevelt said, "It is hard to fail, but it is worse never to have tried to succeed." What goal are you striving to accomplish this year? Do you think that you will succeed? Why or why not?

Conversation #52

What past accomplishment makes you feel the proudest?

Conversation #53

If you found a magical eraser with the power to eliminate one mistake from your life, what blunder would you undo? Why?

Conversation #54

If you could have any superpower, what would it be? How would you use this power for good?

Conversation #55

Have you been the victim of bullying? If so, what happened? Do you wish that you had handled this situation any differently? If so, what would you change?

Conversation #56

Finish this sentence: "Something every teenager should know about dating is _____."

Conversation #57

In your opinion, what is one of the best family vacations we have taken so far? What made this time so meaningful to you?

Conversation #58

What kind of vacations would you like to take in the future?

Conversation #59

In your opinion, what is the primary difficulty that teenagers face today?

Conversation #60

What is the toughest challenge that you currently face? What can I do to support you as you strive to overcome this obstacle?

Conversation #61

Complete this sentence: "Three of the most important people in my life are _____." What are some ways these people add value to your life?

Conversation #62

Complete this sentence: "Something I am looking forward to in the future is _____."

Conversation #63

In your opinion, why do some teenagers use illegal drugs or abuse prescription drugs?

Conversation #64

What is your personal opinion about gun control issues? What causes you to feel this way?

Conversation #65

What should a teenager do if he or she suspects a peer has brought a gun to school?

Conversation #66

In your opinion, what makes teenagers so upset that they engage in random shootings? What are some better ways these teens could handle their anger?

Conversation #67

Superman is archenemies with Lex Luthor. Batman faces off with the Joker. Do you have a nemesis? If so, who is it and what puts the two of you at odds?

Conversation #68

What is your favorite hobby, and how does this activity make you feel?

Conversation #69

If you could change one rule in our home, what would it be? Why would you want to make this change?

Conversation #70

When I notice that you are mad, what would you like me to do?

Conversation #71

In your opinion, what makes our home a fantastic place to live?

Conversation #72

In your opinion, what is one thing that makes our home a frustrating place to live?

Conversation #73

What is the most adventurous thing you have ever done? How did this activity make you feel? Would you do it again?

Conversation #74

Charles Kettering said, "Believe and act as if it were impossible to fail." If you knew that failure was impossible and success was inevitable, what big goal would you attempt?

Conversation #75

What do you (or did you) like least about middle school or high school?

Conversation #76

Finish this sentence: "Something significant that happened to me over the last week was _____. This is important to me because _____."

Conversation #77

What is one significant skill that you gained from your dad?

Conversation #78

What is something helpful that you learned from your grandparents? (This can be something they taught you or something that you discovered by observing them.)

Conversation #79

What is one valuable thing that you learned from your mom?

Conversation #80

Share something significant that you have learned about money and finances. This can come from personal experience or from your observation of others.

Conversation #81

If your life were turned into a book, what would be a good title for your story?

Conversation #82

Pick one of the seven dwarfs to describe how you feel today. Are you most like Happy, Sleepy, Sneezy, Bashful, Dopey, Grumpy, Bashful, or Doc? Explain your answer.

Conversation #83

Share something important that you have learned about dating. This can come from your personal experiences or from your observations of friends and peers.

Conversation #84

When facing a difficult challenge, whom do you look to for wisdom? What makes these people worth seeking advice from?

Conversation #85

The baseball legend, Babe Ruth, said, "Every strike brings me closer to the next home run." Describe a minor mistake that taught you an invaluable lesson. First, describe what happened. Then, explain what you learned from the experience.

Conversation #86

Now, describe a major blunder that made you wiser. First, tell the story of how this blunder came about. Then, explain what the experience taught you.

Conversation #87

If your life were a book, in what section of the bookstore would it be found? Possible answers include the adventure section, sports, drama, comedy, mystery, thrillers, children's books, romance, puzzle books, comics, horror, self-help, science fiction, etc. Explain the reasoning behind your answer.

Conversation #88

Marthe Troly-Curtin said, "Time you enjoy wasting is not wasted time." Using as much detail as possible, describe your ideal weekend.

Conversation #89

What character quality are you striving to develop this year? What makes you want to grow in this area?

Conversation #90

Imagine you find a magic lamp. The genie inside offers to grant you three wishes. However, some restrictions apply. Your first wish must be a selfish wish. This means you must wish for something that will chiefly benefit you. The genie also informs you that wishing for more wishes is strictly forbidden. What is your first wish?

Conversation #91

The genie informs you that your second wish must primarily benefit your family, and once again, wishing for more wishing is off limits. What will your second wish be?

Conversation #92

After rubbing the lamp for the third time, the genie announces that your last request must be for something that will benefit a friend. How will you use your third and final wish?

Conversation #93

Describe your family using characters from the Winnie the Pooh stories. Whom in your family do the following characters best depict?

- Piglet: Timid and easily frightened.
- Tigger: Energetic and adventurous.
- Owl: Full of wisdom.
- Rabbit: Nervous and highly responsible.
- Kanga: Caring and nurturing.
- Pooh Bear: Calm, friendly, and clueless.
- Roo: The baby whom everyone looks after.
- Gopher: A busy builder or workaholic.
- Eeyore: The pessimist of the family.
- A Heffalump: Intimidating.
- A Woolsle: A sneaky troublemaker.
- Christopher Robin: The leader of the bunch.

Conversation #94

Using the Winnie the Pooh characters described above, what would you like your role in your family to be? What changes would you need to make for your family to perceive you this way?

Conversation #95

Which Winnie the Pooh character best represents how your friends identify you? Why do you think that your friends see you this way?

Conversation #96

Describe, in as much detail as possible, how you would like your friends to think of you.

Conversation #97

Katrina Mayer wrote, "The day she let go of the things that were weighing her down, was the day she began to shine the brightest." What past hurts or stresses continue to weigh you down? How will you release them?

Conversation #98

When you feel stressed, what helps you to relax, unwind, and calm down the most?

Conversation #99

What is the greatest joy in your life currently?

Conversation #100

When I make a big mistake, how would you like me to tell you about it?

Conversation #101

When I notice that you are stressed, what should I not do? (i.e., play the stereo loudly, turn off your favorite television show, pretend like nothing is wrong, ask you about it right away, etc.)

Conversation #102

What is one of your happiest childhood memories? What made this time so special for you?

Conversation #103

What is one of your happiest teenage memories — or one of the happiest memories so far? What made this time awesome?

Conversation #104

What new hobby or activity would you like to try this year?

Conversation #105

What is your opinion about teenage alcohol use? Explain the reasons for your answer.

Conversation #106

What is your personal opinion about drinking alcohol as an adult? Explain your answer.

Conversation #107

In your opinion, what are some good things about dating when you are a teenager?

Conversation #108

In your opinion, what are some potentially negative aspects of dating when you are a teenager?

Conversation #109

In your opinion, is it possible for teenagers to enjoy the positive aspects of dating and to avoid the negative ones? If so, how might this be accomplished?

Conversation #110

Finish this sentence: "A good story about me that I have not told you happened when _____."

Conversation #111

Aristotle said, "We are what we repeatedly do. Excellence, then, is not an act, but a habit." What is one habit of excellence you are building into your life?

Conversation #112

If you had a magic wand that could alter one thing about your physical appearance, what would you change, and why?

Conversation #113

If a life coach offered to help you improve one area of your life, what would you ask this person to help you improve?

Conversation #114

Name three things that are good about being you.

Conversation #115

What is your earliest childhood memory — the very first one that comes to mind?

Conversation #116

In your opinion, what does it take to have a good marriage?

Conversation #117

In your opinion, what qualities make you (or will make you) a good spouse?

Conversation #118

Finish this sentence: "In my opinion, a husband and wife should never _____."

Conversation #119

Finish this sentence: "In my opinion, a husband and wife should often _____."

Conversation #120

What is your favorite holiday, and what do you like about it?

Conversation #121

Share a happy memory from your favorite holiday.

Conversation #122

In your opinion, what should teenagers and parents do when they are having a tough time getting along?

Conversation #123

Think back to an argument you had in the past. Briefly describe the event, then share one thing that you wish you had done differently.

Conversation #124

If you could vacation anywhere in the world, where would it be, and why?

Conversation #125

Imagine you just won a million dollars. What will your first purchase be?

Conversation #126

Imagine a rich relative passes away, leaving you in charge of managing his estate. Your first task is to donate one hundred thousand dollars of his fortune to any charity you choose. Which cause do you donate to, and why?

Conversation #127

Do you know a hurting person that our family could help? How might we be an encouragement to this person?

Conversation #128

Describe one way that your friends positively influence you.

Conversation #129

Describe a way that your friends negatively influence you—or have tried to negatively influence you in the past.

Conversation #130

In your opinion, what can teenagers do to avoid negative peer pressure?

Conversation #131

Now that we have completed the conversation starters in this book, how will we continue to connect with each other?

Connecting
In a Disconnected World

The weary engine of the church bus sputtered as we rolled to a stop. Nearly fifty rowdy teenagers rose to their feet and scrambled through the narrow exit. After hours of being tightly packed together, two and sometimes three to a seat, everybody was eager to spread out. Our youth group was on its way to a weekend retreat when engine trouble brought our journey to a halt. This, however, was no surprise. In fact, it happened often enough for our leaders to joke, "It's not a real youth event unless the bus breaks down."

Fortunately, the adults were well prepared. The bus was taken to a nearby repair shop while our youth pastor led us to a grassy lawn to wait. Over the next three hours, we picnicked, played impromptu games of football, chatted, and just hung out. Once the bus was fixed—or at least running well enough to complete the next leg of our journey—everyone scrambled back inside, and the trip resumed.

Although our group was the last to arrive at the retreat, I overheard some kids suggest that we had the most fun, and this may have been the case. Without a doubt, the lengthy dose of unstructured time together had formed us into a tightly knit group.

After a weekend packed with goofy games, speaker presentations, and plenty of time to hang out, our youth group began the trek home. No one was surprised when the rickety old bus broke down a second time. Because the sun was setting and the repair shops were closed, we spent that night in a hotel. There were more impromptu games of football, practical jokes, and an abundance of free time.

Barriers to Happiness

As a teenager, I thought that boredom was horrific. I viewed the world as an exciting place, and in my mind being bored meant that I was missing out. Today, I understand that boredom is not nearly as miserable as most teenagers believe. In fact, boredom can serve as a catalyst for creative ideas, exploration, and adventure.

It was a dull, rainy day when Lucy wandered into the wardrobe and discovered Narnia. Monotony set in shortly before Alice fell down the rabbit hole and entered Wonderland. Moreover, in the Harry Potter series, Harry finds himself either locked in his room or assigned the most tedious of tasks before the adventures begin. These fairy tales reflect a real-life truth: adventures sneak up on us when we least expect it!

I experienced this in our church youth group. I made friends, participated in new activities, and stepped outside of my comfort zone because there was nothing else to do, and this led to much joy! Sadly, in our fast-paced, high-tech society, a profusion of distractions is now a barrier to these powerful connection moments. Studies show that the increased use of electronic devices is contributing to a lack of face-to-face interactions. This has stirred up a host of problems for our teens.

Face-to-Face Happiness

Face-to-face interactions reduce stress, elevate happiness, and help teenagers to stay emotionally balanced. I was fortunate to have grown up in an era where these types of connections came easily. Had I been born twenty-five years later, my teenage years would have been far more entertaining, and I would have been less happy as a result. As it turns out, happiness can be counterintuitive. Often, the things that teenagers think they want actually end up robbing them of joy.

In effect, teenagers with electronic devices, including smartphones, tablets, and laptop computers, are a lot like toddlers given free rein in a candy store. At first, the sweets bring pure delight. After a while, subtle stomach rumblings signal that it would be a good idea to stop devouring the sweets. If these warnings are ignored, then consequences follow. First, a sugar crash sets in. This is followed by a sour mood and a severe tummy ache. As we will see, toddlers, teenagers, and many adults for that matter, place their desires for immediate gratification above actions that lead to long-term happiness. They just do not understand what brings lasting joy.

The Teen Mental Health Epidemic

A study conducted by San Diego State and Florida State University found that "adolescents who spent more time on new media (including social media and electronic devices such as smartphones) were more likely to report mental health issues, and adolescents who spent more time on nonscreen activities (in-person social interaction, sports/exercise, homework, print media, and attending religious services) were less likely."[5] According to this research, 2010 marked the end of an era where mental health problems steadily declined. Then, between 2010-2015, there was a sudden spike in mental health issues, with 33% more adolescents exhibiting high levels of depressive symptoms than in previous years.

During this period, the smartphone craze intensified. In 2012, about half of Americans used smartphones. However, by 2015, 92% of teenagers owned smartphones.[5] As teenagers spent more time on electronic devices, they spent less time in face-to-face conversations, reading print books, participating in sports, exercising, and attending religious services. Because of this, their happiness declined.

In early 2015, I spoke to a local youth pastor and shared how significant my church youth group had been to me. I told him that I longed to find an active youth group for my daughters. His face dropped as he declared, "We only run a few events each year. Nowadays, teenagers are so busy that it is nearly impossible to get them to show up." He reported that this is a rising trend among churches. At the time, I had difficulty accepting this. Yet, the data reinforces his statement. Today's teenagers are both busier and more disconnected than previous generations.

Sadly, this makes perfect sense. As a teenager, I would have loved our modern smartphones, tablets, and laptop computers. Had I been able to play video games, text friends, and watch movies with such ease, I would have been far less eager to explore the world. Like a toddler in a candy store, I would not have known when to stop.

Fortunately, in 1996, the year I graduated from high school, dial-up connections kept the online world cumbersome. Few of my friends had ever been on the internet, and face-to-face relationships were the norm. Undoubtedly, our word has changed. High-tech devices are here to stay, bringing both new advantages and novel challenges. As we have already seen, increased screen time results in fewer face-to-face interactions, leading to a rise in teenage mental health problems. The bright side is that today's teenagers also have more opportunities than ever before.

These same devices also allow teenagers to publish books, start blogs, begin online businesses, and actively engage in charitable works. Many of these opportunities were not available a mere decade ago. Consequently, my outlook is hopeful. Teenagers do not need adults to declare war on screen time. However, they can benefit from increased guidance, as it is possible to navigate this new era with grace. Perhaps the best way to accomplish this is to direct teens toward more face-to-face conversations — which is what this book is all about.

When my wife, Jenny, was a child, her parents would order her to go outside and tell her not to come back in until they called for her. Jenny's face lights up whenever she tells this story, even while she describes how frustrated she felt at the time. It is easy to see that the hours she spent exploring, connecting with friends, and reading in a tree mean a lot to her today. Your teenagers may have a similar experience. While they may not fully appreciate face-to-face connection now, it is likely they will one day look back and see just how meaningful these times were.

The bottom line is that face-to-face relationships matter, so it is imperative to keep connecting with your teen. Because you and your teen are continually changing, there are always new conversations to have. The research shows that this is what our teens need, and your teenager may appreciate it more than you realize. I wish you and your teen many more engaging conversations in the years ahead!

End Notes

1. Holt-Lunstad Julianne, Layton Bradley, Smith Timothy, "Social Relationships and Mortality Risk: A Meta-analytic Review." PLOS Medicine, July 27, 2010: http://journals.plos.org/plosmedicine/article?id=10.1371/journal.pmed.1000316

2. Miner, Maureen. "The Impact of Child-Parent Attachment, Attachment to God and Religious Orientation on Psychological Adjustment." *Journal of Psychology and Theology* 37.2 (2009): 114-24. *ProQuest.* Web. 15 Dec. 2013.

3. Genesis 2:23.

4. Ecclesiastes 4:10

5. Twenge J.M, Martin G.N, Joiner T.E, and Rogers M.L. "Increases in Depressive Symptoms, Suicide-Related Outcomes, and Suicide Rates among U.S. Adolescents After 2010 and Links to Increased New Media Screen Time." *Clinical Psychological Science* 6, no. 1 (2018): 3–17.

Thumbs Up
or Thumbs Down

Thank you for purchasing this book!

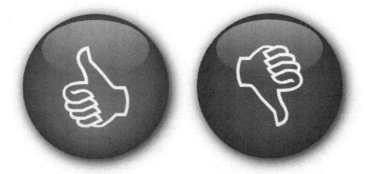

I would love to hear from you! Your feedback not only helps me grow as a writer, but it also helps me to get books into the hands of those who need them most. Online reviews are one of the most significant ways that independent authors—like me—connect with new readers.

If you loved the book, could you please share your experience? Leaving feedback is as easy as answering any of these questions:

- What did you like about the book?

- What is your most valuable takeaway from this book?
- What have you done differently—or what will you do differently because of what you have read?
- To whom would you recommend this book?

Of course, I am looking for honest reviews. So if you have a minute to share your experience, good or bad, please consider leaving a review!

I look forward to hearing from you!

Sincerely, Jed Jurchenko

About the Author

Jed is passionate about helping people live happy, healthy, more connected lives by having better conversations. He is a husband, father of four girls, a psychology professor, therapist, and writer.

Jed graduated from Southern California Seminary with a Master of Divinity and returned to complete a second master's degree in psychology. In his free time, Jed enjoys walking on the beach, reading, and spending time with his incredible family.

Continue the Conversation

If you enjoyed this book, I would love it if you would leave a review. Your feedback is an enormous encouragement to me, and it helps books like this one to get noticed. It only takes a minute, and every review is much appreciated. Oh, and please feel free to stay in touch too!

E-mail: jed@coffeeshopconversations.com

Twitter: @jjurchenko

Facebook: **Coffee Shop Conversations**

Blog: **www.CoffeeeShopConversations.com**

More Family Books

This book and other creative conversation starters are available at www.Amazon.com.

Transform your relationship from dull and bland to inspired, passionate, and connected as you grow your insights into your spouse's inner world! Whether you are newly dating or nearing your golden anniversary, these questions are for you! This book will help you share your heart and dive into your partner's inner world.

131 Conversations for Couples

More Family Books

These creative conversation starters will inspire your kids to pause their electronics, grow their social skills, and develop lifelong relationships!

This book is for children and tweens who desire to build face-to-face connections and everyone who wants to help their kids to connect in an increasingly disconnected world. Get your kids talking with this activity book the entire family will enjoy.

131 Conversations That Engage Kids

Made in the USA
San Bernardino, CA
11 July 2019